I Will Fly
A Collection of Poems

Florence Ndiyah

Langaa Research & Publishing CIG
Mankon, Bamenda

Publisher
Langaa RPCIG
Langaa Research & Publishing Common Initiative Group
P.O. Box 902 Mankon
Bamenda
North West Region
Cameroon
Langaagrp@gmail.com
www.langaa-rpcig.net

Distributed in and outside N. America by African Books Collective
orders@africanbookscollective.com
www.africanbookcollective.com

ISBN: 9956-726-22-2

DISCLAIMER
All views expressed in this publication are those of the author and do
not necessarily reflect the views of Langaa RPCIG.

Dedication

To Rev. Fr. John B. Ambe

Table of Contents

Preface

I Will Fly is a collection of 52 poems which bring to life a story of struggle and hope.

It opens with a first set of poems on difficulties faced by Cameroonian citizens. The characters fall in two groups: First, ordinary Cameroonians who simply cannot make ends meet, who daily entertain hardship. Unemployment, underemployment and related consequences darken their general demeanour. The second group are English-speaking Cameroonians. As the minority population, they constantly bear the weight of marginalisation. Incessant struggle often bears desperation.

However, the Cameroonian society is not all about dearth. While some live on crumbs, others squander, like buying items they do not need. Conflict arises: The poor cannot stand the thriftlessness of the rich while the rich condemn the poor for their indolence and jealousy.

Protests. The people have had enough. But what next after the protests, which unfortunately, do not always satisfy the whims of the protesters. Several options: Some resign; they give up, ready to accept whatever comes. At times this constitutes nothing. They just have to wait. Waiting causes stillness.

Others search for an escape route through travel. The youth would sell a head for a chance to get out, to fly far away. Civil servants seek the pleasure of holidays from embezzled funds. Some simply catch and follow the strings which their spouses hurl from abroad. Even the old want to go. Many don the aprons of babysitters to mind their grandchildren.

They go but the dreamland does not always fulfil its promises. Some who settle abroad adopt identity issues. Many never return home though their new "homes" never really accept them. They live there but never belong. African in skin yet Western in culture. Something always betrays them. Others who return home can't find their place. The affluent impose the presence of dollars and euros and pounds. The tongue, the foreign accent, becomes the anchor of others.

Immigration is not the only escape outlet for exasperated Cameroonians. Another group see solace in death. Nevertheless, whatever death does, irrespective of how many people invite it and how many more times it comes uninvited, it never conquers.

Death is too unappealing an option for others, the adventurers. While for some adventure comes as part of the job description, others adopt it to spice up their lives. The troubled mothers of the reckless, exhausted from trying to reason with their children, just sit home and wait for them to return, upright or inclined.

Still some distressed citizens take refuge in romance. Some, the women, see marriage as a way out. Yet while some seek bounding with every nerve in their bodies, others treasure singlehood. Still others, young men, especially the lazy ones, take to selling themselves. Some just have fun, the men like the women. They forget their problems in relationships. In the process some emit the victory laugh while others are left with bleeding wounds which refuse to heal.

Hope. It's never far away from the minds of all these individuals. Hope in the future. Hope cultured through religion. Hope. There is hope for a better life, for a better nation, for a better Africa.

Florence Ndiyah

Book I

Part 1: For Food in a Spoon

The Burden of Sight

Fruits spread on side roads
Saliva for our dry throats.
Myriad quarries still whole
We burrow into rat-holes.
Our lawns invaded by stranded oaks
Floors bear our plates of disowned oats.
Plastic eyes, pearls we could own
Would give us little reason to moan.

10/02/07

Brains in Bottles

Idleness grows on my fingers nails,
Perfect clasp for my beer bottles
Bought with borrowed dough
Debt to my weary mother
Should I go horizontal
Before I prove I was vertical.

Like an unfertilised egg
A brain like mine,
Fed with the finest
Abandoned with the emptiest.
Decomposing,
While still I walk,
Standing on feet
With a head fed to maggots.

Like an unfertilised egg,
A beggar in a bar
Colleague to drunkards.
No footprints to mark my passage
Like someone who was never born.

15/02/08

Blackout

I open my eyes and all I see is black,
The horizon rushed out to meet me
Greet me,
And eat me!
Choked by its proximity,
Lost in its infinity.

I'm all alone in the dark,
A monstrous silhouette on the walls
Behind the dying candle flame.
I wish to hear the banging on the door
Of a visitor hand,
Talking for the dumb bell.
Company,
Another silhouette to chase me away
From the walls.

I wish for the noise of the rain
Hail dancing on the roof.
But only dead silence with me,
Like in the world of the sleeping.
Where is the day
With the music of birds?
They're all gone.
If I could just hear them sleep!

They're all gone,
No newswoman, the voice on the radio,
Announcing the contraction of night.
Even the droning of my old refrigerator
That often left me yelling.
Oh,
How I wish for it,
The life of light,
Power!

The absence of power
Not such a dread as in days past,
When my refrigerator challenged supermarkets.
Trashed with two such days.
Now just a monument,
A reminder of the life of old.

The absence of power
A mirror of days to come.
The lonely shelves in my refrigerator,
The darkness and silence
Walk me
To the land of the sleeping.

21/06/08

Part 2: Toxic English

Anglo!

Colonial tongues
Stunt our growth.
English, the wrong language,
Like one which came in through the back door.

They walk ahead,
Open our front doors,
Usher us into our homes and
Make us fast at our feasts.

Aware,
Yet appalled every time it happens again.
We return to that first time with the hope
Of denuding what was garbed then.
Naked beldams! The sun refuses to rise.

Lilliputians,
Our limitation stands out,
Towering above us,
Dragging us to places we'd rather not go.

12/11/07

A Questionable Prescription in My Mouth

I swallow
The tablet that used to calm my headache.
Fallouts I get,
Not relief.
The tablet,
It's still whole
But the medicine is no longer in it.
It's only excipient.
I've become resistant
Not to medicine
But to excipient.

The tablet calmed my headache
Before it lost its power.
Spew it out?
The medicine may return.
Swallow on,
I remain sick.
What am I to do?

08/01/08

The Dark Side of Night

I'm afraid to close my eyes
Lest the night take over my soul
Give me its eyes,
And make me see the dark side of night.

It's like I live in the underground,
The ground layer of the earth;
Buried there in the basement
Like a man who wakes in a coffin.

I'm like a lost memory
Forgotten in the profound depth of a brain;
Unable to breath
Chocking inside layers of tight cells,
Unable to remember
What true living is;
For something shelters me
From the goodness of life.
It protects me
From laughter and joy,
Friendship and happiness.
It confines me to itself
Like someone in an old picture
Trapped in a metal frame.

My life has become a scary scene
Which comes to life from a book,
It takes a little shape each day
Until it convinces me it's real
And shares everything with me
Like a loving partner.

24/06/09

P for Presbytery, Priest and People

A house with transparent brick walls
Vigilant eyes
And very flippant mouth.
Where the entry of each stray fly is documented
And presented to the big master in the immediate present
Lest nightfall dulls the details.

A glimpse into the corridor
Through the door standing ajar,
Like an open invitation.
But bars of invisible steel
Chill the skin of the "intruder"
And stop blood running down their feet.

A house built for a man of the people,

To receive the people;
But only those with iron hands
Dare lift the steel bars
To get across to the promised land.

The bronze coins that fell from common hands
Erected a palace not fit for common feet.
And so many look on from a distance
At the extraordinary house
Built from their ordinary means.
13/11/08

Concealed Tracks

That land once so familiar
Has become like foreign soil.
Yet its specks stick to their soles
And follow them about,
Calling them to return
To that land of their sweat.

Once it was a place of peace;
A kind good morning
To a nameless face
Certain it was one of theirs.
Now it's rowdy like a battlefield,

Foreign languages
Rising to drown the silence.

It used to be the only place
Outside of their homes,
Where English was master
Even to the weirdest stranger.
Now it's a place
Where English is the stranger
And her daughters roam about hopelessly,
Wondering if they will ever find
Their way home,
To that place where God awaits them.

13/11/08

God's Israel

Enslaved in our own land
Persecuted by our own hands
Lured by the tune of pagan bands
To resisting our Creator's wand.

Undesired like stubborn weed,
We roamed about in hostile field
Waiting for God to take the lead

14

Our hearts and pockets He filled.

Planted like the tower of Babel
We headed for the heavenly border
With neglect to the God of our fathers
Who delivered us from much oppression.

Dispersed to foreign altars
We are scattered about
Like the twelve tribes of Israel
Yearning for our Redeemer.

Yet His love ever-faithful,
Prophets He harvests from our midst.
So we better go back on our knees
And keep track behind His heels.

15/11/08

Book II

Waste

A Noiseless Phone

She'll stare at it from dawn to dusk
And wonder why it just can't ring
She bangs its case and taps its tusk
But nothing like that simple ding.

She'll hide it in her thick blanket
And listen to the radio sing
But her toes hit the hard gadget
And make her bid that thing to ting.

A clock that cannot chime the time
And lets her sleep without its beep
Now she is left with not a dime
But just a phone that makes her weep.

10/11/07

Book III

Accusation

You Sink the Nation

His a life of yearn and yawn:
Loose sandals eaten by tar,
Flimsy frame follows the wind.
Four solid limbs!
He could sow them and harvest his wants,
Amass some mass and fight the wind.
He, a disciple of dearth.

Hers a life of pick and pay:
Stilettos eating up the tar,
Ornamented bulk barring the wind.
Dirty money!
Chokes on gifts larger than spouse's payslip
And curses him for giving too little.
She, a prisoner of property.

They walk past,
Shoulders touch, necks twirl,
Eyes lock in critical stare.
Pity measures up with pity
Then it flashes away
Like it had never lived
In those two damning stares.

09/02/07

23

Book IV

Protests

Stocking Up For Protest Days

A drop of ocean in a pot of water
Leaves grains of beans salty.
A drop of ocean, life to dry fish,
Poison in oil spill.
With fire, water and oil marry
Their love burning on candles,
Light that dispels darkness.

25/02/08

27

The Country Is Not People

The country is not people
Only a name over a piece of land.
The paths by our homes are not lanes
Just heavily guarded borders.
The youths on the streets are not flesh
But wood,
Sap flowing from their bullet wounds.

The country could be people.

27/02/08

No Golden Eggcups for the Morrow

Eggs in silver eggcups on the breakfast table
Keep me awake in my sleep;
And even as butter is melting in my mouth
I'm already gazing at three slices of meat,
Mountains on my green plate of vegetables.
No space for many waiting mangoes
And supper with a new taste from another pot.

A silk bow at the back, Cinderella's ball gown,
My Christmas dress.
Simple and pure, a Snow White dress
For the New Year.
Soon June and I will be folding my nice clothes;
Off to the province to flaunt capital vogue.
Stuff in more play clothes,
Trousers to go up mango trees
And gowns to play 'Mother'.
Folklore by the fireside with grandma
For two months after June.

No good report card, no holidays!
Papa has never been soft on that.
Better eat my eggs and get some proteins
To catch all the lessons of Miss Molten,
And someday decide how I holiday.

I will be big like a baobab tree,
My branches banknotes
That will buy me greenness and freshness.
I need to age fast, money grow with me.
A banker like Papa but with a bigger purse.
Age come fast with prosperity on your back
And golden eggcups on my breakfast table.

But the gunshots stalk me,
And kill my dreams
With bullets in my blackboard.
I look into the holes and all I see are shadows.
The loud explosions silence the songs of the birds
That I meet at the treetop by the sky.
Even when I am up near the sky,
All I see is the ground.

'Splattered shrapnel,
Mines maiming,
The devil beneath the earth!'
Big words.
Now a caption in daddy's morning paper
Soon to be a chapter in my history book.
If I will ever hold a book again
If I will ever grow big.

05/11/07

Book V

Part 1: Resignation

Holy Dust

She wouldn't water her yard before sweeping
For there'll be more dust when she goes tilling.
She covers her nose and sweeps up to the wall
And prays for God to quickly send rainfall.

He wouldn't wash the dust off his dirty lorry
Since it'll just pile up and make him sorry.
He uses the wipers, whistles and looks ahead
For the day God sends aid to tar the dust bed.

Even with their immaculate white garments
They wouldn't dust the bench segments.
Since it's church and they just need to pray
And God cares only about what they'll say.

02/02/07

Wait

When I don't know what to do
I do nothing.
I wait.
When I can't get what I want
I get what I can.
I simply wait:
For the moment to pass
For another day to come
For the desire to wait to be dispelled.
I can't say what I wait for
But I know I wait;
And at times I have to wait and wait
For some 'waits' really last long.
Yet I know that after the wait
I will have no reason to wait again
And no reason to ask why I did not wait.

Numbed initiate,
Inferior will?
I watch time walking away from me,
Heading to a place I can't go.
I watch it go with the eyes of a statue.

14/04/09

Still

The rivers have become lakes.
The wind has lost its limbs.
The flames, they are quiet,
Like a shy house,
Low, simple,
Close to the ground.
Silent,
Still
All is still!

Like a city ashamed of itself,
Cowers before its contemporaries,
Its reflection swallowed by the earth.
Invisible!
Nothing to catch the eyes and make them roam for more,
Nothing to exact a smile.

When will the water run again,
The wind walk and talk,
The flames dance to the tune of the crackling wood?
When will the house stand up
And multiply itself around the city?
When will life come into everything?
09/08/09

Part 2: Escape

Section One: Immigration

I Will Fly

I will sit on the air,
Cross borders without landmarks,
Move further and further from home
Until I know not where I roam.

I will sleep on the air,
Wake between dancing clouds
Enveloped in their mist, I'll hove,
"Ah! So I'm finally above."

I will go where my feet freeze,
Where bus wheels wheeze,
And the ship sails fail.
I will go where the birds go.

Someday, I will steal my tuition fee,
Trade my brother's inheritance,
And even indebt my progeny.
One day, I will own my flying fee.

I too will climb those hanging stairs.
I too will meet the rainbow up there.
I too will find land where the road ends.
I too will fly.
18/11/08

A Dream Too Far

He took me from home
With promises to quiet my moan,
Show me life I'd never known
If I just follow his hand.

I packed away my history books
And picked up a new slate
To start writing another story
In colours
Brighter than I had ever used.

Now my days are longer
My hours idlers
And my dread greater.
No better bread
No redder meat.
Just spring and snow,
Elements I can live without.

Hunger for home
Creates voids not filled even by love.
Dead, all the glittering promises.
Chained in a present I wish I never knew.

21/03/09

Leave

Leave to search for life in lands far off.
Lifeless beings on strange shores
The journey's end.

Leave to crush foreign sand beneath my feet,
No thought to what lies therein:
The last breath of compatriots chased away by my
benefactor
Or life-changing steps for countless hungry youths.

Life is mine.
Why bend to look below when I can stretch and pluck
from above,
My back held up by the state.

Leave.
Time for me to leave my desk,
To stand up and keeping walking
As far as bank figures can take me.
Leave. The chance to live with Guicci and Yves
In Hilton and Sheraton.

My treasure the "matricule",
The gem the government offers me
Permission to take without asking,

41

And go as far as I can see
Till Columbus bids me stop,
No place new to discover.

Leave.
Interspaced by seminars.
Leave behind the shorts and shirts
For suits and ties,
My place to find
In the world of decisions.
Push the case of my state
Sell my people,
Return home to a promotion;
More figures to take me further
On my next leave.

4/12/11

Grandmother's Luggage

That time we raced with the falcons,
Remember?
Strapped on seats, sleeping
But floating through the heavens,
Soaring into nothingness.

64kg of luggage to stay balanced,
But you sided with gravity
In your plans to move Africa to America.
Parcels, parcels and more parcels
Of home-grown delicacies
From anyone who voiced a familiar name:
For Jenka'a; for Wakuna; for Kah

Egusi and Eru, njangsa and janga –
As I stuffed your compassion into our suitcases,
You were weighed down by worries
Of how the packets will arrive doorsteps.
"Well, once they have crossed seas
They will certainly cross streets,"
You consoled.

Soon I will again be your staff
Supporting you over Africa and across America.
Who knows what will pull us earthward this time.

You have already sighed about Kristel and Dwayne,
More props of your grandchildren.
You have grumbled that Andin and her American man
Did not send home for Nahbila and Babila.
Would names be part of our luggage this time?

15/02/07

Treacherous Hands

A black woman
Walks a homeless white dog
Down a brown street.

A creased hand holds the leash
Like one which grew by a fireside
Wrinkled by harsh amber flames.

With knuckles hard and charred
Resistant as placenta stains
To anti-melanin lotions.

Her complexion imprisoned
In empty bottles of whitening creams
Floating in dark septic tanks.

A furless dog has no colour
No name, no owner, no home
Like a hand with two colours.

06/09/08

On Once Familiar Streets

Streets stare at the black strands
Knotted up behind my head,
And hear them say:
"Takes half a century for
Blacks to grow a ponytail.
Your mother,
With a white man
Must have been charitable
With genetic secretions."

Slight, high, bright –
That's me creation feeds to their eyes.
"Feed flesh onto your brittle bones;
You're a skeletal sculpture.
No room for magazine girls
On our hills,"
My plump maternity
Taunt me each homecoming.

They search me
For the little girl from their memory.
That's the me they know.
That's the me they want.
She's not coming back.
She's gone.

05/01/06

Paper beyond Papers

Painted in various colours,
Of sizes unrelated to value,
The fuel that enables man,
Which gives him reason
To walk, sleep and dream.
Multiply multiples,
The mission of many who walk the earth.

Not how much space it occupies
In the trunk of the car.
That's too narrow an estimation of its worth.
Sitting on the palm,
Small and silent
Yet bigger than the trunks of five cars filled,
The little gadget it acquires.

Enfolded by fingers,
The fate of families for decades
It could change.

Floating shoulders
Held up by paper;
Sink into the neck
At the sight of determined breeze.
Yet they embrace the paper,
Cling to it like it comes with the weight of five cars;
Splash it around
Like it was plucked from their gardens,
Watered with a hose
Filled from the spring.

Paper, that's all it is;
Yet papers they be not.

07/12/11

Section Two: Mortality

Quitting By the Fast Lane

There the jobless go for sprees,
Where bikes become buzzing bees,
Which head out from every corner
And scamper into every bunker.

Swinging on exhibition seat,
The speed of rushing cars to beat,
On tight streets with pitted ways
And leaking sides on rainy days.

The headlights of a car at night,
Two bikes emitting the same light;
They crash into the number plate
And take many to a sorry fate.

Riders who love the sight of gore,
And hate the lives of even more,
Mount another three on their backs
And chase big cars on fast tracks.

Broken bones and bruised skin,
Chilled bodies next to wailing kin:
Daily records in hospital files
From riders revving battle cries.
10/09/08

A Song of Many Pitches

When all is joy, the laugh is wide
Shared with loved ones by the side,
Where there is little to hide
And so much to pride.

The news hits like a hammer on a nail
Causing an enormous wail,
Accompanied by drops like eager rain,
That attempt so vain.

At times it be high in pitch
Like the wail of a bitch
Making the throat itch
As though it required a stitch.

Sometimes it be low, lame
Like a man defeated in his game,
Full of shame
For bearing part of the blame.

More times a heavy sigh,
The silent cry with many a why
Of the going of one with hopes so high
Left without a final goodbye.
15/11/04

The Doomed Day

Who would have thought
That the day will come
When I will tell you goodnight
And keep vigil while you sleep on,
Then walk away and leave you there?

Who would have thought
That I will talk on while you listen;
Yet listening will be all you will do
Since you'll be unable to talk back;
That even my tears
Will leave you indifferent?

Who would have thought,
That many would gather
Not to laugh with you
But to cry on you,
Not to consult you
But to impose on you.
And yes,
You will have no say at all?

Who would have thought it?
I always knew it could happen
But I thought it was still far away,

That it was going to give us time.
I knew it could happen
When I... when we ...
I knew it could happen
But never that it will be this real.

13/11/04

No Glory in the Morning

A tender shoot of Morning Glory,
Boon to the dying garden,
Blooms with hopeful colour.

But the dooming noon sun,
Soon sears its roots.
Withered and barren
It droops.

Sooty and teary the clouds of night
Too late for the shoot.
The lonely, crescent moon,
The mouth humming the dirge

Soon another morning
But without yesterday's glory

Only the purple,
The sad reminder.

10/11/07

The Snail Shell

Someday,
Someone will point to a spot
On the ground.
There I will be buried
There I will lie
Year after year
For more years than I lived
For more years than man lives.

Next to eternity,
These few years I live
Stand like the shadow of a single wrinkle
On a snail shell.
Deeper and heavier it becomes
As each year mounts on the other
Though they be just figures.

Those figures I love to bury
Hide them even from me.

Their sight a spiteful reminder
Of beauty on a fast walk
To the spot on the ground
Through the snail shell.

Someday I will be a shell
Which has never been smooth
Which has never know beauty,
A shell,
Empty.

03/07/09

That Little House at the End of the Road

That house with no windows
And with just one small door.
That house built only for one
That claustrophobic little house.

That house below the earth
With address above the earth.
That house in which day is night
That sombre little house.

That house which the affluent dread
The only one they refuse to own
But which obstinately stalks them
That determined little house.

That house with indifferent neighbours
Where rare visitors are left unattended
That house trampled beneath feet.
That horizontal little house

19/10/04

Enemy in the Shadows

You stride in a non-invitee
Yet you will leave with a big souvenir.
Relaxed, never in a haste
One with such a refined taste.
Though you claim a thousand trophies a day
You will never be the winner so gay,
For each time you knock one to the ground
Two come forth with a welcoming sound.

25/01/05

Part 3: Adventure

Behind My Camera

They stand at attention in front of flags;
I scurry about, reserves films in my bags.
They honour the dead with a minute of silence;
To capture the moment, I fidget without pretence.
They discard body parts in their quest for shelter;
A new arm, my camera, I edge towards danger.

I rewind the past to enrich the present.
I eternise history: Mandela is President.
I grab time and bid it stand still.
I clutch age and pin it down at will.
I ignite desire in lonely hearts of love.
I'm memory! I'm evidence! I'm love!

But obsession with my passion carries a sentence:
Any moment be honoured with a minute of silence.

04/02/07

61

Indispensable Intruders

Those fingers which dial "emergency"
When the underworld cut off your phone line.
Those fast feet which appear with assistance
When your flag is up with an S......O.......S.
Those empathetic mouths which bear witness
To the truth of your innocence.

But

Those curious ears which stick to your walls
And suck up scraps of your closet stories.
Those prying eyes which follow your shadow
Even when you shut them out with opaque blinds.
Those sharp noses that inhale your hot oven
And trail it right to your dinner table.

Yes

They are the blisters in your new trainers
And the iodine that heals your fresh wound.
They are the nicotine in your cigar sticks
That swells your ego but kill your body.
They are present even when your breath flees
They who are faithful like death.
20/02/07

Poet's Block

Poem
Where are you?
I roam about my room ready
With pen
And pad whose ears are bigger than mine,
Taking no chances
Lest you come and slip away.

Come now,
When I can capture you,
Not a dream at night
When I'll have to skip up and switch on
And grope around for pen and paper
Only to spell steel steal.

Come now,
Not at joint with buddies
When I'll have to brand you by beer bottles
Or steal away
To avoid the tag
"Shakespeare everywhere".
Come now!
You who say I catch an ant and count its feet
And explain the world without words;
You who say I state the taste of my tongue

And tell the smell of my nose.
You who say I see a toad
As a toddler with dog bone stuck in throat.

Come now.
I need you now
When I can hear the footsteps of ants and
See Shigella straight.
Come now with those lines that'll
Make a damsel see a rough rock as red rose
Whose petals lead her to my door
To show me the feel of touch.

Come now poem
And live on my page.

16/11/07

The Words of Women

Some women's words
Are like flippant corpses.
Though silent, they convey a message,
One which makes sense
Only to a select few,
But brings the downfall
Of multitudes.

Some women's words
Are like people who travel
A long journey from the past,
Who skip generations,
To invade the present
And mess it up.

Some women are louder than birds
Which come to commune uninvited,
Dancing on roof tops
And singing from window panes.

Some women don't have a voice.
They take refuge in signs.
Simple gestures
Yet heavy casualties they cause.
25/06/09

Leave The Door Open

We sit and fold our arms in front of televisions
Unaware they are out offering streets huge embraces.
Learning we provide them to explore their visions,
They use to swing our errors on their old shoelaces.
We fill their rubber plates with our mothers' recipes
And watch them empty their souls to our friends' stares.
School shocks? Love burns? In their wars for peace
They push us to the back to protect us from nightmares.
We provoke dialogue but they parade gloomy moods
And shrink our fears with big words from their books.

The path of impatience may lead to radiant sunrise
If only they find its trail which vanishes with sunset.
Loh is now squatting in a dark alley with starved mice,
Aching for his favourite smoke-smelling *fufu*, that I bet.
His nocturnal wails for milk pull the bedcovers off me.
At the window, the night gets creepier with each tick
Flitting images of spiced chicken on china tempt me
Television pictures swallowed only by the unrealistic.
One day he will see that the road nowhere leads home.
To cots or in coffins, it always starts and ends at home.

01/02/07

Part 4: Romance

Living in Him

To know he goes to sleep with me,
The air in his arms
Trapped between his body and the sheets,
Mine the lips against his on the pillow
Be in his head so hard I'm in his bed.
That's all I want,
For now.

To know he opens his eyes with me,
That he feels me before he sees the new day,
The cold that attacks his body,
Leaves him wondering how to fight back.
To know he sees me on his bare table
And the empty pots in his kitchen.

It's not ideal
But it's sufficient,
For now.
Resting and staying there in his head,
Miles apart but never far away,
Closer than even his thoughts.

14/12/07

Three Women in a Pair of Shoes

They who've walked the path of men,
Hold my hand and pull me back
To the days before the Beijing Conference and
The Ministry of Women's Affairs.

"Abuse your diet but don't make it a habit;
Break a glass, the one you will replace.
Just do something but say nothing.
Say nothing, that is the secret,"
They say.

Mothers of our fathers,
Bonded to strangers
Achieved the silver
Their mantra:
"Say nothing!"

"Say nothing, that's the secret,"
"Pretence," I ask.
They raise their hands
And shake their heads.
"Respect!"

Guinea pig:
Is it working?

Is it worth it?
"The fashion of a today's woman
Holds half the truth as collateral."

16/01/07

The Woman in Me

She glares like glass in bright sunlight
And flares like flames in bars of gold.
She is joyful like a day born at the right time
And peaceful like a sky which sleeps with stars.

The prominent Queen of the Night,
She is confident like a full moon at midnight
And evident like a burning mountain,
Mirrored in the twilight glow of the sky.

Light like a leaf that follows the gentle breeze,
She rises with the doves toward the rainbow,
Surging undisturbed to gracious heights
Until she reaches the peak of the world.

17/03/09

Unattached and Unavailable

If I show them my fur
They will call me another dog.
Spartans,
They flatter and sway gold in my face
But I prefer the weightlessness of air.
Sketch cupid on his wife's arm,
Peek into my eyes and
Bid me desert my skin and dwell in hers.

If I pluck off my feathers
They will call me another chicken.
They comb me for nakedness.
My bare finger:
Their triumph and their threat.
In my eyes, their reflections
As they cuddle their husbands,
Those ghostly possessions.

It is something strange to me
All the smiles
That used to be there for me
Now there are whys and sighs
Just waiting for me.
How I became the enemy
Whom they team up to attack

Each for a personal reason.

19/01/08

G'glo

The aggressive nudity of a Greek god
Mirror of ferocity of our aroused dog
Roaming her house like a live-in stud
Those who run from living by the spud

Little reflection about precaution
It approaches the area of seclusion
Three orifices fervently tempting
One to receive the flush emptying

Completely relieved of its sanity
It delves into the vacant cavity
And with the rhythm of a throb
It vigorously executes the job

The darting dick dips deeper
Filling up, conquering the inner
With monotonous routine motion
Till flowing fluid frees the tension

With the satisfaction of the flaccid member

Evaporate the promises never to remember

Which lived only long as the rowdy ecstasy

When pleasure rowdily echoed – oh Stacy!

12/09/04

Saturday Evening with Girlfriends

"How many men have you known?"

To a man whose mouth is full of spit,

I'm Helen of Troy

Steel in his stare.

To a David,

I'm Jezebel

As I read Ruth on his lips,

The example of his great-grandmother.

"How many men have you known?"

They ask for an inventory

When all they care

Is to multiply the stock.

I will go to my girlfriends

They are more reliable than love.

We will eat out and watch movies,

Not the romance realities in which we are veteran stars
But comedies that will make us forget we are women.
We will choose the best restaurant,
Look boisterous as spinsters.
Men will think we are on their trail.
Women will disown us.

"How many men have you known?"
We will hijack a man to sit behind us,
Bleed his pockets
To make up for his brothers' misdeed.
Send him home a misogynist
Minus one mouth to ask:
"How many men have you known?"

19/2/07

From Brother To Brother

How girls bother.
Don't talk, brother.
Merciless.
Shameless.
Double-dealers!
Gold-diggers!

Silence

Must all be of the same mother.
Born on the same day, brother.
Like an angel on the first day,
The devil after a short stay,
Arousing the man in you.
Poisoning all love in you.

Silence

What's your story?
Makes me feel sorry.
Mine's cheating.
She left me bleeding.
With my best friend.
With my worst fiend.

Sighing

What did you do?
What could I do?
Throw her out?
Let her hang about?
I so miss her dimple
Crater for my pimple

Nervous laughter

Toyed with her dreadlocks.
Many come with braided locks.
Hers, natural ones on brown hair.
Dimples, dreadlocks, brown hair?
Dimples, dreadlocks, brown...Wait!
No! No! No! I came first. You wait!

Exclaim together

Susan!

10/02/07

Oh Woman

Without woman, what is man?
Born and nurtured by woman
Though both of them human.

The boy, the man, of substance same
Draining her warmth, igniting her flame
As they cling to her soft, soothing frame

Who is she, the woman of his life:
His mother, teaching him to hold a knife?
The mother of his children, his dear wife?

They both dedicate their womanhood
One moulding him through childhood,
The other supporting him in manhood.

Without woman man is nothing
With woman man is everything
United they produce something.

25/09/04

The Longest March

Footsteps without prints
I leave nothing behind
As I take that long walk
On a very short distance.

My mother,
Pushing me forward
I've been too slow.
My father,
Holding me back,
No man worth his queen.
Squashed in-between,
I can't tell if I'm moving at all.

I want to arrive, but not too fast
Lest I seem too eager.
I want to arrive but not too slowly,
Lest another girl overtake me.
I want to be there
Just on time.

It's not my feet that tell me I've arrived
It's my eyes
His in mine
In the last step.

That day I'm a queen
Walking a royal road.

We start a journey;
I hold his hand
He holds my hand.
Neither knows where we are going
Only He who is leading
Those two hands in one.
Guided by the many hands that join the chain
As we walk the way.

21/03/09

Part 5: Hope

Awakening the Stars

Some days appear premature,
Arriving before their due date,
Like they mistakenly dropped off the calendar
Before God had finished with them.

Some days are so black
It's like they were born
Before God fashioned the sun
And commanded it to light up the earth.
Such days ignore the light
And stubbornly go on
To their ill ends.

But even in the essence of the dark
When light rays seem too big
To penetrate the pores of darkness,
God is present in that sad day,
Another of His creations.

In the night of that darkness
They who look carefully
Will be sure to see God's hand
Holding up the stars,
Preventing them from falling off
To be buried in the earth's core.

Sit To Stand

Day and it flies over earth
A straw on its beak
To supplement brother's efforts
At building a nest for the young.
Noon and it pecks on crumbs
Singing between meals.
Night and it perches on a branch.
I see it and I desire it:
The peace of a bird.

Claiming its share of the road,
It emerges to play with friend,
Dines on an old bone,
And naps on the lawn.
I see it in the dog:
Its freedom and simplicity;
And I want it.

They file in from wonderland
Bearing parcels;
Anything but worries they be,
Surely rations for the inactive.

A kiss for every mouth on the way.
I see the love and unity of ants
And I yearn for it.

I see the creatures of the world
Loving and supportive
Never knowing what they will nibble next
But always knowing their mouths will not be idle;
Never knowing where they will lay their heads
But always knowing they will not go to sleep on their feet.
I see them,
I admire them
And I want to be like them.

05/09/06

I Want Never To Wish For Yesterday

I want never to wish for yesterday
Since tomorrow will lend me some wings
If I let today use my feet.

I want never to wish for yesterday
For it is now dead and buried
Present only as mental pictures.

I want never to wish for yesterday
Only that tomorrow be like yesterday
A new day with the old victories in better wrappings.

I know today is soon to be another yesterday
So I make it live in me and through me,
A solid foundation for a better tomorrow.

I want never to wish for yesterday
Since tomorrow will lend me some wings
If I let today use my feet.

05/07/09

Toss To a Friend

I don't know how tonight is going to die
But I know I'm going to be
Needing you more and more.

I don't know where tomorrow is going to be
But I know I'm going to be
Loving you more and more.

It's a love that just can't cease.
The only certainty of my life,
This love that keeps my breath flowing.

At the end of the day
It is to you I come
With all my secrets
A safe dwelling to create
Shaded from the light of day.

At the end of it all
You the one who hold my hand
That which I do not offer
And take me to that place I long to go
Though at times I fail to know.

You the one who complete me

Not like they who compete with me
With the aim to deplete me
In our search for the completion point.

You the one who guide me
In my search for the completion point.

05/07/09

No Need for a Rocket

At times the strength seems so far away
On eagle wings.
But most often it just there,
At the tip of my fingers,
Just waiting for the push.

Sometimes the next step
Seems on the wheels of racing cars;
Yet most often it's just there
At the end of my feet, getting set,
Just waiting for "go".

Many times the right word
Seems so hard to find
But most often it's just there

At the tip of my tongue
Just waiting to claim sound.

We don't have to own a rocket
Or get into a cannon
To land where the sun rises.
Most often the sun is right there,
Rising in the east of our beings.

04/12/08

Now I Remember How to Pray

There are times when
I forget how to pray.
"God knows all I need
And
I take all He gives."

But then I remember,
Not exactly how to pray
But how to say
"Thank you".

I remember
How sweet it is to call His name,
To send a lullaby up to heaven,
To welcome the sun with a song.

I remember
How to beg on behalf of my neighbour,
And how to remind Him
Of that which I know He hasn't forgotten.

I remember
My need for salvation.
Suddenly
Gravity pulls my knees down

And I unite with my God
In prayer.

Life is one long prayer,
Said with open eyes
On walking feet
By an active mouth
In a crammed place.

The day we realise
That we had been praying
In the midst of the beehive,
That day we stop praying.

So we keep moving
With our eyes open,
Following life
Going about its business
But praying all the while.

23/11/08

Book VI

Light for Africa

Black and Gold

It is dark as black:
Disease eating deep into its marrow;
Forsaking the living for the welfare of the un-conceived;
Thinking with one head yet claiming to speak for the
people;
Selling its kindred for a few pieces of bronze;
Transforming its territory into a warehouse of vices.

Yet it is bright as gold,
Richly blest with natures best:
Heritage, a gift from generations past;
Culture, anchor in a drifting world;
Wisdom, the effect of faith;
Hospitality, smiles for strangers;
People, the height of wealth;
And gold, the symbol of its heart.

Though black be on the surface
With gold buried deep in the core
Resolve brings them together;
The black highlighting the gold
The gold disguising the black.
Either way, that is what it is:
Black and gold,
The promise untold.